LIGHTNING BOLT BOOKS™

What Holds Us to Earth?
A Look at Gravity

Jennifer Boothroyd

Lerner Publications Company
Minneapolis

To my
special friend
Emily—
who keeps her feet
on the ground and
her head in the
clouds

Lerner Publications Company
A division of Lerner Publishing Group, Inc.
241 First Avenue North
Minneapolis, MN 55401 U.S.A.

Website address: www.lernerbooks.com

Library of Congress Cataloging-in-Publication Data

Boothroyd, Jennifer, 1972–
        What holds us to earth? : a look at gravity / by Jennifer Boothroyd.
            p.   cm. — (Lightning bolt books™—Exploring Physical Science)
        Includes index.
        ISBN 978-0-7613-5430-7 (lib. bdg. : alk. paper)
        1. Gravity—Juvenile literature. I. Title.
        QC178.B634 2011
        531'.14—dc22   2009038499

Manufactured in the United States of America
1 — BP — 7/15/10

Contents

Something is Different

Look at this picture. Does something look out of place?

You are right! This woman is floating in the air.

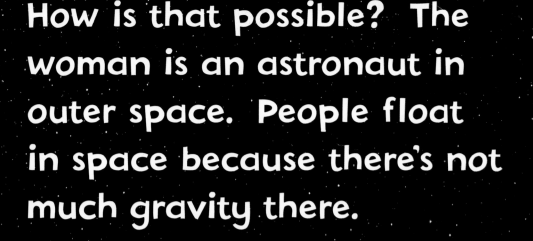

How is that possible? The woman is an astronaut in outer space. People float in space because there's not much gravity there.

Outer space has only a little bit of gravity. Astronauts call it microgravity. Micro means "very little."

A Strong Pull

Gravity is a force. It pulls things toward the center of Earth.

A force is a push or a pull. A ball falls to the ground when you drop it because of gravity's pull.

You cannot see gravity. But you can see how it affects things. It pulls on waterfalls. It pulls on falling leaves. It pulls a boy down a slide.

Watch out! A plate will fall to the floor if you drop it. Gravity makes objects fall until something stops them.

The hard floor will stop a dropped plate from falling. And gravity will keep the plate on the floor.

Without gravity, the pieces of this broken plate would float away!

9

Hey, batter, batter! Swing!
This batter hits the ball hard.

The force of her bat is stronger than gravity.

The ball soars high in the air.

A thrown baseball would fall to the ground if the force from a bat didn't make it soar.

But wait! The force from the bat is weakening. Gravity is pulling the ball down. A player waits to catch it.

When a player catches a ball, she stops gravity from pulling the ball down to Earth.

Center of Gravity

Gravity helps things balance. Everything has a center of gravity. A center of gravity is a balancing point.

This model seesaw's center of gravity is at the center of the board. The seesaw can balance if it's supported at its center.

Gravity pulls equally on an object's center of gravity. That's why objects can stay balanced if they're supported at this point.

This pencil can stay balanced because it's supported at its center of gravity.

Gravity In Space

Gravity's pull helps us live on Earth. It keeps water from floating away. It lets things stay in place.

Many people's drinking water comes from lakes and streams. If we didn't have gravity, this water would float away!

Other objects in space also have gravity.

Objects with more mass
have more gravity.
Mass is the amount of
matter in an object.

The sun has a lot of mass.
The sun's gravity is very strong.

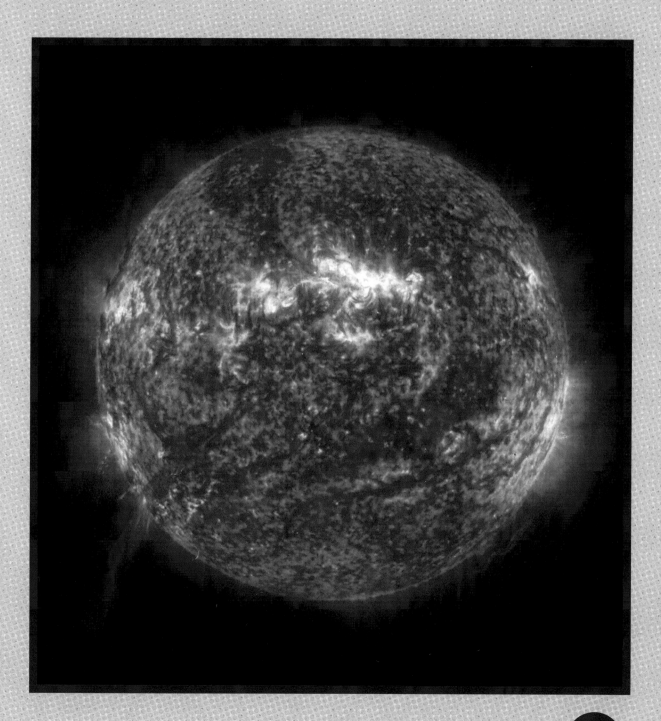

The moon has little mass.

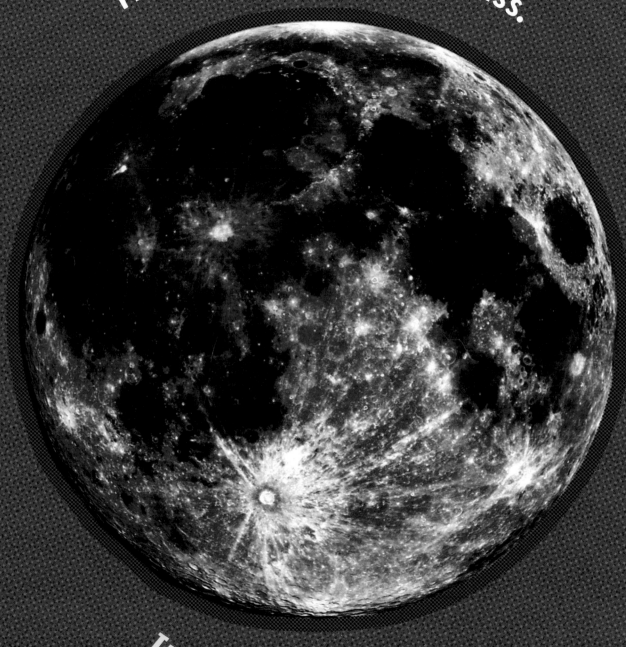

Its gravity is weak.

Astronauts bounce and float when they walk on the moon!

Astronaut Edgar Mitchell walked on the moon in 1971.

What Is Weight?

How much do you weigh? Your weight is how much gravity pulls on your body.

This scooter weighs about 180 pounds (82 kilograms). On Earth, you weigh less than this scooter. Gravity pulls on the scooter more.

Imagine you visit the moon with the scooter. Both you and the scooter have the same mass as you did on Earth. You didn't lose any parts!

But on the moon, the scooter weighs about 30 pounds (14 kg). You weigh even less. Since there's less gravity on the moon than on Earth, things weigh less on the moon.

Floating through Life

Do you remember the astronaut at the beginning of this book? Astronauts need to learn how to live with little gravity.

They need to learn to hold
onto things in space, or the
things will float away.

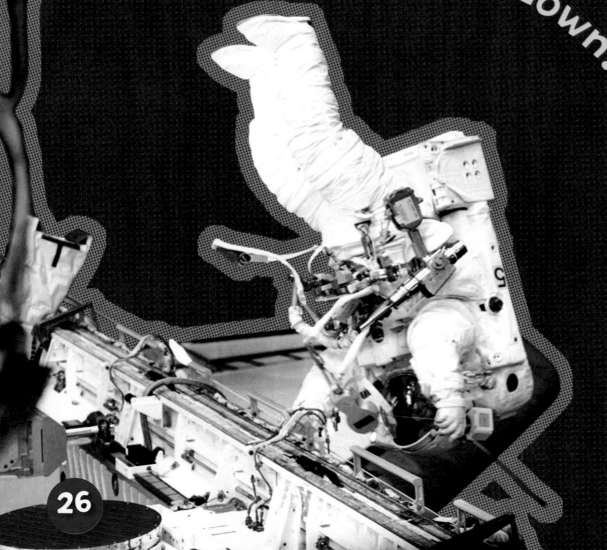

Astronauts even need to learn how to work upside down!

Take a look around you.
Gravity is everywhere.
Can you imagine your
life without it?

27

Activity
Galileo's Drop

Galileo Galilei was a scientist in the 1600s. He discovered that gravity makes objects fall at the same speed no matter their weight. Follow these steps to try an experiment like Galileo's.

What you need:
a cookie sheet
a table
a baseball
a tennis ball

What you do:

1. Place the cookie sheet on the floor at the edge of the table.

2. Take the baseball in one hand and the tennis ball in the other. Then hold the balls over the cookie sheet while resting your wrists on the table's edge. The table will help you keep your hands steady and even. That way, you'll be sure that you're dropping the balls from the same height.

3. Drop the balls at the same time. When they land, you'll hear them hit the cookie sheet. The noise will help you know for sure which ball landed first.

So which ball landed first? Or was it a tie? Were the results of your experiment the same as Galileo's?

Glossary

astronaut: someone who travels in space

center of gravity: a point where an object balances

force: a push or a pull

gravity: a force that pulls things down toward the surface of Earth

mass: the amount of matter in an object

matter: what things are made of

Further Reading

Boothroyd, Jennifer. *Give It a Push! Give It a Pull!: A Look at Forces.* Minneapolis: Lerner Publications Company, 2011.

Branley, Franklyn M. *Gravity Is a Mystery.* New York: Collins, 2007.

Dragonfly TV: Microgravity
http://pbskids.org/dragonflytv/show/microgravity.html

Hopwood, James. *Cool Gravity Activities: Fun Science Projects about Balance.* Edina, MN: Abdo, 2008.

Science of Baseball: The Scientific Slugger
http://exploratorium.edu/baseball/scientificslugger.html

Your Weight on Other Worlds
http://www.exploratorium.edu/ronh/weight/index.html

Index

Photo Acknowledgments

The images in this book are used with the permission of: © Alan Bailey/Getty Images, p. 2; NASA, pp. 4, 24, 25; © Barry Blackman/SuperStock, p. 5; © Bellurget Jean Louis/ Stock Image/Getty Images, p. 6; © iStockphoto.com/mammamaart, p.6 (inset); © DK Stock/David Deas/Getty Images, p. 7; © Shannon Fagan/The Image Bank/Getty Images, p. 8; © Flirt/SuperStock, p. 9; © Flip Chalfant/The Image Bank/Getty Images, p. 10; © Rob Atkins/Photographer's Choice/Getty Images, p. 11; © John Burcham/National Geographic/Getty Images, p. 12; © Westend61/SuperStock, p. 13; © Brand New Images/ Stone/Getty Images, p. 14; © iStockphoto.com/Robert Dupuis, p. 15; NASA and The Hubble Heritage Team (STScI/AURA), p. 16; SOHO – EIT Consortium, ESA, NASA, p. 17; © iStockphoto.com/Rafael Pacheco, p. 18; NASA/JSC, p. 19; © image100/Alamy, p. 20; © iStockphoto.com/Hedda Gjerpen, pp. 21, 23 (inset right); © Prisma/SuperStock, p. 22; NASA/MSFC, pp. 23 (background), 26; © Dave King/Getty Images, p. 23 (inset left); © Chris Windsor/Taxi/Getty Images, p. 27; © Lew Robertson/StockFood Creative/Getty Images, p. 28 (cookie sheet); © Sam Lund/Independent Picture Service, p. 28 (baseball); © iStockphoto.com/Daniel Cooper, p. 28 (tennis ball); © iStockphoto.com/Don Nichols, p. 28 (table); © Photodisc/Getty Images, p. 30; © Chuck Franklin/Alamy, p. 31.

Front cover: © David Ball/Alamy